EASY STIR FRY COOKBOOK

50 UNIQUE STIR FRY RECIPES

2nd Edition

By
Chef Maggie Chow
Copyright © 2015 by Saxonberg Associates
All rights reserved

Published by
BookSumo, a division of Saxonberg Associates
http://www.booksumo.com/

STAY TO THE END OF THE COOKBOOK AND RECEIVE....

I really appreciate when people, take the time to read all of my recipes.

So, as a gift for reading this entire cookbook you will receive a **massive collection of special recipes.**

Read to the end of this cookbook and get my ***Easy Specialty Cookbook Box Set for FREE***!

This box set includes the following:

   1. ***Easy Sushi Cookbook***

2. ***Easy Dump Dinner Cookbook***
3. ***Easy Beans Cookbook***

Remember this box set is about **EASY** cooking.

In the ***Easy Sushi Cookbook*** you will learn the easiest methods to prepare almost every type of Japanese Sushi i.e. *California Rolls, the Perfect Sushi Rice, Crab Rolls, Osaka Style Sushi*, and so many others.

Then we go on to *Dump Dinners*. Nothing can be easier than a Dump Dinner. In the ***Easy Dump Dinner Cookbook*** we will learn how to master our slow cookers and make some amazingly unique dinners that will take almost ***no effort***.

Finally in the ***Easy Beans Cookbook*** we tackle one of my favorite side dishes: Beans. There are so many delicious ways to make Baked Beans and Bean Salads that I had to share them.

So stay till the end and then keep on cooking with my *Easy Specialty Cookbook Box Set*!

About the Author.

Maggie Chow is the author and creator of your favorite *Easy Cookbooks* and *The Effortless Chef Series*. Maggie is a lover of all things related to food. Maggie loves nothing more than finding new recipes, trying them out, and then making them her own, by adding or removing ingredients, tweaking cooking times, and anything to make the recipe not only taste better, but be easier to cook!

For a complete listing of all my books please see my author page.

INTRODUCTION

Welcome to *The Effortless Chef Series*! Thank you for taking the time to download the *Easy Stir Fry Cookbook*. Come take a journey with me into the delights of easy cooking. The point of this cookbook and all my cookbooks is to exemplify the effortless nature of cooking simply.

In this book we focus on delicious stir fry recipes that are simple and unique. You will find that even though the recipes are simple, the taste of the dishes is quite amazing.

So will you join me in an adventure of simple cooking? If the answer is yes (and I hope it is) please consult the table of contents to find the dishes you are most interested in. Once you are ready jump right in and start cooking.

— Chef Maggie Chow

Table of Contents

Stay To the End of the Cookbook and Receive.... 2
About the Author.................................. 5
Introduction 7
Table of Contents 8
Any Issues? Contact Me 12
Legal Notes.. 13
Chapter 1: Easy Stir Fry Recipes.......... 14
   The Easiest Veggie Stir-Fry 14
   A Japanese Stir-Fry.......................... 17
   Pork Loin Stir Fry 20
   The Best Chicken Stir-Fry I Know ... 24
   Oriental Stir-Fry 27
   A Texas-Mexican Stir Fry................. 30
   Jerk Stir-Fry..................................... 33
   (Caribbean) 33

- Beef Stir-Fry I 36
- Asparagus Stir-Fry 39
- Beef Stir-Fry II 41
- Almond Stir Fry 44
- Orange-Chicken Stir Fry 47
- Tomato and Egg Stir Fry 50
- Tofu Stir Fry..................................... 52
- Chicken And Lemon Stir-Fry 55
- A Turkey Stir-Fry 58
- Tofu Stir Fry II 61
- Pork Stir Fry II 64
- Sesame Veggie Stir-Fry 67
- Bitter Melon Stir-Fry........................ 70
- Indian Stir-Fry 73
- Ragin' Cajun Stir-Fry 76
- Cabbage Stir-Fry 80
- Bok Choy Stir-Fry 82
- Asparagus Stir-Fry Re-Imagined..... 84
- Maggie's Favorite Shrimp Stir-Fry.. 87
- Ginger Pork Stir Fry......................... 90

Mediterranean Stir-Fry 93
Chicken and Garlic 96
Lemon and Shrimp Stir Fry 99
(Paleo Approved) 99
Chinese Skirt Steak Stir Fry 102
Pork and Tofu Stir Fry 105
Indian Style Tofu with Lime Stir Fry
.... 108
Grapes and Chicken 111
Easy Hawaiian Stir Fry 113
Mexican Style Pork Stir Fry 116
Every Pepper Stir Fry 119
Couscous and Cauliflower Stir Fry 122
Easy Eggplant and Spinach Stir Fry
.... 125
Watermelon and Pepper Stir-Fry .. 128
Down South Stir Fry 131
Vietnamese Stir-Fry 134
Filipino Style Steak Stir Fry 138
Chicken and Spaghetti Stir Fry 141
Caribbean Stir Fry 144

Maggie's Easy Shrimp and Garlic.. 147

Ginger Tofu with Peanut Sauce 150

Orange Chicken and Broccoli II 153

Chinese Pork 156

Easy Stir Fry Lo Mein 159

Ginger Chicken with Apricots 163

THANKS FOR READING! NOW LET'S TRY SOME **SUSHI** AND **DUMP DINNERS**....
.... 166

Come On... 168

Let's Be Friends :) 168

Can I Ask A Favour? 169

Interested in Other Easy Cookbooks?
.... 170

Any Issues? Contact Me

If you find that something important to you is missing from this book please contact me at maggie@booksumo.com.

I will try my best to re-publish a revised copy taking your feedback into consideration and let you know when the book has been revised with you in mind.

:)

— Chef Maggie Chow

LEGAL NOTES

ALL RIGHTS RESERVED. NO PART OF THIS BOOK MAY BE REPRODUCED OR TRANSMITTED IN ANY FORM OR BY ANY MEANS. PHOTOCOPYING, POSTING ONLINE, AND / OR DIGITAL COPYING IS STRICTLY PROHIBITED UNLESS WRITTEN PERMISSION IS GRANTED BY THE BOOK'S PUBLISHING COMPANY. LIMITED USE OF THE BOOK'S TEXT IS PERMITTED FOR USE IN REVIEWS WRITTEN FOR THE PUBLIC AND/OR PUBLIC DOMAIN.

Chapter 1: Easy Stir Fry Recipes

The Easiest Veggie Stir-Fry

Ingredients

- 2 tbsps soy sauce
- 1 tbsp brown sugar
- 2 tsps garlic powder
- 2 tsps peanut butter
- 2 tsps olive oil
- 1 (16 ounce) package frozen mixed vegetables

Directions

- Get a bowl and combine the following ingredients: peanut butter, say sauce, garlic powder, and brown sugar.
- Grab a wok and heat your oil.
- Now begin to fry your veggies for 7 mins.

- Before serving season the veggies with some soy sauce.
- Enjoy

Servings: 6 servings

Timing Information:

Preparation	Cooking	Total Time
5 mins	5 mins	10 mins

Nutritional Information:

Calories	88 kcal
Carbohydrates	13.8 g
Cholesterol	0 mg
Fat	2.9 g
Fiber	3.3 g
Protein	3.5 g
Sodium	345 mg

* Percent Daily Values are based on a 2,000 calorie diet.

A Japanese Stir-Fry

Ingredients

- 2 pounds boneless beef sirloin or beef top round steaks (3/4" thick)
- 3 tbsps cornstarch
- 1 (10.5 ounce) can Campbell's® Condensed Beef Broth
- 1/2 cup soy sauce
- 2 tbsps sugar
- 2 tbsps vegetable oil
- 4 cups sliced shiitake mushrooms
- 1 head Chinese cabbage (bok choy), thinly sliced
- 2 medium red peppers, cut into 2"-long strips
- 3 stalks celery, sliced
- 2 medium green onions, cut into 2" pieces
- Hot cooked regular long-grain white rice

Directions

- To start this recipe grab a knife and begin to cut your beef into some thin long strips.
- Grab a medium sized bowl and combine the following ingredients: sugar, broth, soy, and cornstarch.
- After combining the ingredients let the contents rest for a bit.
- Get your wok hot over a high level of heat and add one 1 tbsp of oil to it. Allow the oil to heat up as well.
- Once your oil is hot combine the following ingredients in it: green onions, mushrooms, celery, cabbage, and peppers.
- Fry these veggies down until you find that they are soft. Once soft remove them from the heat.
- Now grab your cornstarch mixture and put it in the pot fry and continually stir until you find that it has thicken.
- Once thick combine the cornstarch with your beef and veggies. Fry until beef is cooked completely.
- Let contents cool.
- Enjoy.

Servings: 8 servings

Timing Information:

Preparation	Cooking	Total Time
30 mins	15 mins	45 mins

Nutritional Information:

Calories	290 kcal
Carbohydrates	26.4 g
Cholesterol	39 mg
Fat	7.6 g
Fiber	2.6 g
Protein	26.4 g
Sodium	1271 mg

* Percent Daily Values are based on a 2,000 calorie diet.

Pork Loin Stir Fry

Ingredients

Marinade:

- 1/4 cup rice wine vinegar
- 2 tbsps minced garlic
- 1 tbsp brown sugar
- 5 tbsps olive oil
- salt and pepper to taste

Stir Fry:

- 4 boneless pork loin chops, cut into bite sized pieces
- 5 tbsps vegetable oil
- 3 tbsps finely chopped fresh ginger root
- 1 tbsp hot chile paste
- 5 tbsps teriyaki sauce
- 1 green bell pepper, cut into strips
- 1 red bell pepper, cut into strips
- 1 yellow bell pepper, cut into strips
- salt and pepper to taste

- 1/4 cup blanched slivered almonds
- 2 tbsps chopped fresh mint

Directions

- Grab a bowl, and combine the following ingredients: salt and pepper, rice wine vinegar, olive oil, garlic, and brown sugar.
- Mix the ingredients together for a minute then mix in your pieces of pork.
- Place a cover over the bowl and let the pork marinate for about 30 minutes.
- Heat a wok with a medium level of heat.
- Fry almonds until they emit a wonderful aroma.
- Add oil to the almonds and get it hot.
- Fry pork, chili paste, and ginger.
- Add teriyaki sauce, and stir-fry vigorously, with high heat, until pork cooked fully.
- Add peppers, continue frying until no liquid left.
- Garnish with mint.

- Enjoy.

Servings: 4 servings

Timing Information:

Preparation	Cooking	Total Time
30 mins	10 mins	1 hr 10 mins

Nutritional Information:

Calories	579 kcal
Carbohydrates	17.5 g
Cholesterol	59 mg
Fat	45.1 g
Fiber	2.2 g
Protein	27.5 g
Sodium	935 mg

* Percent Daily Values are based on a 2,000 calorie diet.

THE BEST CHICKEN STIR-FRY I KNOW

Ingredients

- 2 cups white rice
- 4 cups water
- 2/3 cup soy sauce
- 1/4 cup brown sugar
- 1 tbsp cornstarch
- 1 tbsp minced fresh ginger
- 1 tbsp minced garlic
- 1/4 tsp red pepper flakes
- 3 skinless, boneless chicken breast halves, thinly sliced
- 1 tbsp sesame oil
- 1 green bell pepper, cut into matchsticks
- 1 (8 ounce) can sliced water chestnuts, drained
- 1 head broccoli, broken into florets
- 1 cup sliced carrots
- 1 onion, cut into large chunks
- 1 tbsp sesame oil

Directions

- Get a saucepan. Add rice and water. Get water boiling with high heat. Once boiling lower heat to low. Cover and let rice cook for 25 to 30 mins.
- Get a small bowl and mix the following ingredients: corn starch, soy sauce, and brown sugar.
- Combine with the corn starch: red pepper, ginger, and garlic.
- This is your marinade. Cover chicken with it for 30 mins.
- Get a wok heat 1 tbsp of sesame oil hot with high heat.
- Fry the following ingredients for 6 mins: onion, bell pepper, carrots, water chestnuts, and broccoli. Place aside.
- Add 1 tbsp of sesame oil to your frying pan and get it hot.
- Grab your chicken and separate the meat and marinade.
- Fry the chicken for 3 mins on each side until almost cooked but not 100% done.
- Add veggies to the chicken and stir fry everything for 10 mins.
- Enjoy.

Servings: 6 servings

Timing Information:

Preparation	Cooking	Total Time
30 mins	35 mins	1 hr 20 mins

Nutritional Information:

Calories	700 kcal
Carbohydrates	76.7 g
Cholesterol	161 mg
Fat	12.1 g
Fiber	4.9 g
Protein	67.7 g
Sodium	1790 mg

* Percent Daily Values are based on a 2,000 calorie diet.

Oriental Stir-Fry

Ingredients

- 1 (20 ounce) can Pineapple Chunks
- 1/3 cup reduced-sodium soy sauce
- 2 tbsps cornstarch, divided
- 3/4 tsp crushed red pepper
- 3/4 tsp garlic powder
- 1 pound fresh or thawed medium-size shrimp, peeled and deveined
- 1 tbsp reduced-sodium soy sauce
- 2 tbsps vegetable oil
- 1 (16 ounce) package frozen Oriental vegetable medley
- 1 tsp minced fresh ginger
- 4 cups cooked white or brown rice

Directions

- Get your pineapple and remove any liquid. Keep 1/4 cup of pineapple liquid.

- Grab a bowl and combine the following ingredients: 1/2 cup of water, pineapple juice, garlic, 1/3 cup of soy sauce, pepper, and 1 tbsp of cornstarch. Put aside.
- Get another bowl and mix shrimp with soy sauce and cornstarch. Use 1 tbsp of soy and 1 tbsp of cornstarch.
- Get a wok and heat your oil with high heat.
- Fry the shrimp for two mins. Put aside.
- Stir fry ginger and frozen veggies for four mins.
- Mix pineapple shrimp and veggies in wok. Cook everything for 2 mins over high heat.
- Enjoy.

Servings: 4 servings

Timing Information:

Preparation	Cooking	Total Time
10 mins	10 mins	20 mins

Nutritional Information:

Calories	1012 kcal
Carbohydrates	185.6 g
Cholesterol	173 mg
Fat	10.6 g
Fiber	4.7 g
Protein	36.5 g
Sodium	1652 mg

* Percent Daily Values are based on a 2,000 calorie diet.

A Texas-Mexican Stir Fry

Ingredients

- 1 tsp olive oil
- 1 green bell pepper, chopped
- 1 red bell pepper, chopped
- 2 tbsps all-purpose flour, or as needed
- 1 (1 ounce) packet taco seasoning mix
- 1 pound skinless, boneless chicken breast halves, diced
- 2 tsps olive oil
- 1 (15 ounce) can black beans, rinsed and drained
- 1/2 cup prepared salsa
- 1 cup shredded Cheddar cheese

Directions

- Get a skillet, heat 1 tsp olive oil. Fry red and green peppers for 5 mins, remove them.
- Grab a bowl combine the following: taco seasoning and

flour. Add your chicken. Coat the chicken.
- Get your wok. Heat 2 tsps of olive oil. Fry chicken for five mins, until cooked.
- Combine the peppers from earlier with the chicken and also add some salsa, and black beans.
- Stir fry, the chicken, the peppers, the beans, and salsa for 5 mins.
- Serve with cheddar cheese.
- Enjoy.

Servings: 4 servings

Timing Information:

Preparation	Cooking	Total Time
20 mins	15 mins	35 mins

Nutritional Information:

Calories	333 kcal
Carbohydrates	13.3 g
Cholesterol	94 mg
Fat	5.9 g
Fiber	1.7 g
Protein	32.1 g
Sodium	945 mg

* Percent Daily Values are based on a 2,000 calorie diet.

Jerk Stir-Fry

(Caribbean)

Ingredients

- 1 tbsp vegetable oil
- 1 green bell pepper, seeded and cubed
- 1 red bell pepper, seeded and cubed
- 1/4 cup sliced sweet onions
- 3/4 pound skinless, boneless chicken breast, cut into strips
- 2 1/2 tsps Caribbean jerk seasoning
- 1/2 cup plum sauce
- 1 tbsp soy sauce
- 1/4 cup chopped roasted peanuts

Directions

- Get wok, add oil, and for 7 mins stir fry your onions and peppers until they are soft. Once soft remove them from the pan.

- Get a bowl and combine chicken and jerk seasoning. Evenly coat.
- Stir fry chicken until cooked. Then add plum sauce and onions and peppers. Stir fry for five mins after chicken is cooked.
- Add some soy sauce and peanuts.
- Enjoy.

NOTE: Remember that all stir fries go great with rice.

Servings: 2 servings

Timing Information:

Preparation	Cooking	Total Time
15 mins	20 mins	35 mins

Nutritional Information:

Calories	549 kcal
Carbohydrates	41 g
Cholesterol	104 mg
Fat	21.4 g
Fiber	4.7 g
Protein	44.3 g
Sodium	1621 mg

* Percent Daily Values are based on a 2,000 calorie diet.

Beef Stir-Fry I

Ingredients

- 2 cups brown rice
- 4 cups water
- 2 tbsps cornstarch
- 2 tsps white sugar
- 6 tbsps soy sauce
- 1/4 cup white wine
- 1 tbsp minced fresh ginger
- 1 pound boneless beef round steak, cut into thin strips
- 1 tbsp vegetable oil
- 3 cups broccoli florets
- 2 carrots, thinly sliced
- 1 (6 ounce) package frozen pea pods, thawed
- 2 tbsps chopped onion
- 1 (8 ounce) can sliced water chestnuts, undrained
- 1 cup Chinese cabbage
- 2 large heads bok choy, chopped
- 1 tbsp vegetable oil

Directions

- Get a large pan. Add water, heat until boiling. Add rice. Lower heat to low. Cover the pan. Let the rice cook for 40 mins until done.
- Get a bowl combine the following ingredients: soy sauce, cornstarch, wine, and sugar. Mix evenly then add ginger. Add beef to this marinade.
- Get wok. Heat 1 tsp oil for frying. Stir fry for 1 min: onions, broccoli, pea pods, and carrots.
- Mix in: bok choy, Chinese cabbage, and water chestnuts. Place a lid on the pan and let fry for 4 mins.
- Remove everything from pan.
- Add 1 tsp oil to pan and fry beef for 4 mins. Add veggies back and fry for 3 mins.
- Enjoy with rice.

Servings: 4 servings

Timing Information:

Preparation	Cooking	Total Time
10 mins	1 hr	1 hr 10 mins

Nutritional Information:

Calories	665 kcal
Carbohydrates	104.6 g
Cholesterol	39 mg
Fat	13.8 g
Fiber	11.7 g
Protein	30.5 g
Sodium	1594 mg

* Percent Daily Values are based on a 2,000 calorie diet.

Asparagus Stir-Fry

Ingredients

- 1 tbsp butter
- 1/4 sweet onion, chopped
- 1 pound fresh asparagus, trimmed
- 1 tsp chopped roasted garlic
- 2 tsps teriyaki sauce

Directions

- Get a wok. Melt butter and fry onions until soft then mix in garlic and asparagus. Stir fry for 5 mins.
- After 5 mins of frying add your teriyaki sauce and enjoy.

Servings: 4 servings

Timing Information:

Preparation	Cooking	Total Time
10 mins	5 mins	15 mins

Nutritional Information:

Calories	54 kcal
Carbohydrates	5.5 g
Cholesterol	8 mg
Fat	3.1 g
Fiber	2.2 g
Protein	2.8 g
Sodium	382 mg

* Percent Daily Values are based on a 2,000 calorie diet.

Beef Stir-Fry II

Ingredients

- 1 beef bouillon cube
- 1/3 cup boiling water
- 5 tbsps low-sodium soy sauce
- 2 tbsps cornstarch
- 1 tbsp teriyaki sauce
- 2 tsps white sugar
- 1 pound beef round steak, cut into thin strips
- 1 tbsp olive oil
- 1 (16 ounce) package frozen stir-fry vegetables
- 1 (4 ounce) can sliced water chestnuts, undrained

Directions

- Get a pan. Add water. Heat until boiling. Pour hot water into bowl. In the water mix: beef bouillon cube, sugar, soy sauce, teriyaki sauce, and cornstarch.
- Input beef into this mixture and evenly coat.

- Get a wok. Heat oil. Add vegetables and fry for 1 min.
- Add water chestnuts and place a lid on pan. Let everything cook for 5 mins. Remove from pan.
- Fry beef until done for 5 mins.
- Add your veggies back and stir fry everything for two mins.
- Enjoy.

Servings: 4 servings

Timing Information:

Preparation	Cooking	Total Time
10 mins	15 mins	25 mins

Nutritional Information:

Calories	312 kcal
Carbohydrates	24.4 g
Cholesterol	60 mg
Fat	11.7 g
Fiber	4.9 g
Protein	28 g
Sodium	1138 mg

* Percent Daily Values are based on a 2,000 calorie diet.

Almond Stir Fry

Ingredients

- 2 cups water
- 1 cup white rice
- 1 tbsp sesame oil
- 5 cups chopped collard greens
- 1/8 tsp minced garlic
- 1 pinch red pepper flakes, or to taste
- 1/3 cup almonds
- 1 tsp lemon juice, or as needed
- 1 tsp soy sauce
- 1/4 tsp chopped fresh ginger

Directions

- Get a pan. Add water. Heat until boiling. Add rice. Lower heat to low. Place cover over pan. Let cook for 25 to 35 mins until tender (turn off heat).
- Get wok add sesame oil. Fry the following ingredients: red pepper flakes, collard green, and garlic

until you find the collard greens are nice and soft for 10 mins.
- Stir fry the following until no juices remain or 5 mins: the collard greens, almonds, soy sauce, ginger, and lemon juice.
- Let the contents cool. Enjoy.

Servings: 2 servings

Timing Information:

Preparation	Cooking	Total Time
10 mins	35 mins	45 mins

Nutritional Information:

Calories	519 kcal
Carbohydrates	82.8 g
Cholesterol	0 mg
Fat	15.8 g
Fiber	6.4 g
Protein	12.4 g
Sodium	179 mg

* Percent Daily Values are based on a 2,000 calorie diet.

Orange-Chicken Stir Fry

Ingredients

- 1 (16 ounce) package dry whole-wheat noodles
- 1/2 cup chicken stock
- 1/2 cup orange marmalade
- 1/3 cup tamari sauce
- 1 (1 inch) piece ginger root, peeled
- ground black pepper to taste
- 1 lemon, juiced
- 3 tbsps peanut oil
- 2 pounds skinless, boneless chicken breast halves, cut into thin strips
- 1 (16 ounce) bag frozen stir-fry vegetables, thawed

Directions

- Get a pan. Add water and salt. Heat until boiling. Add wheat noodles. Boil for 8 mins. Drain and set aside.

- Get a wok. Add following ingredients fry until sauce thickens: ground black pepper, chicken stock, ginger root piece, tamari sauce, and orange marmalade. Use low heat. Should take 20 mins. Set aside add lemon juice.
- Heat peanut oil in wok. Fry chicken for 6 - 10 mins. Set aside.
- Fry veggies for 5 mins. Add chicken, add sauce. Fry for 2 mins. Remove ginger root.
- Let the contents cool. Serve with your noodles.
- Enjoy.

Servings: 4 servings

Timing Information:

Preparation	Cooking	Total Time
15 mins	45 mins	1 hr

Nutritional Information:

Calories	849 kcal
Carbohydrates	112.5 g
Cholesterol	129 mg
Fat	17.5 g
Fiber	15.7 g
Protein	67.6 g
Sodium	1838 mg

* Percent Daily Values are based on a 2,000 calorie diet.

Tomato and Egg Stir Fry

Ingredients

- 2 tbsps avocado oil, or as needed
- 6 eggs, beaten
- 4 ripe tomatoes, sliced into wedges
- 2 green onions, thinly sliced

Directions

- Get your frying pan hot with medium heat and 1 tbsp of avocado oil.
- Fry your eggs until done around 1 min and plate the eggs
- Add 1 more tbsp of oil in your pan and stir fry tomatoes until dry for around two mins. Now add some onions and begin to re-fry the eggs and onion for half a min.
- Enjoy.

Servings: 3 servings

Timing Information:

Preparation	Cooking	Total Time
10 mins	5 mins	15 mins

Nutritional Information:

Calories	264 kcal
Carbohydrates	9.2 g
Cholesterol	372 mg
Fat	19.7 g
Fiber	2.6 g
Protein	14.5 g
Sodium	151 mg

* Percent Daily Values are based on a 2,000 calorie diet.

Tofu Stir Fry

Ingredients

- 1 (3.5 ounce) package ramen noodles (such as Nissin® Top Ramen)
- 3 tbsps olive oil
- 1 slice firm tofu, cubed
- 1/2 green bell pepper, chopped
- 1/4 small onion, chopped
- 1/3 cup plum sauce
- 1/3 cup sweet and sour sauce

Directions

- Get a pan. Add water and salt. Heat until boiling.
- Use the boiling water to cook your ramen noodles for three mins.
- Get a wok with medium heat get your olive oil hot.
- Fry tofu, onions and pepper for 6 mins.

- The tofu should be on one side of the pan, the onions on another side.
- Combine the ramen with the tofu and peppers.
- Mix in sweet and sour sauce and plum sauce.
- Continue stir frying for three to five mins.
- Let cool and enjoy.

Servings: 2 servings

Timing Information:

Preparation	Cooking	Total Time
10 mins	15 mins	25 mins

Nutritional Information:

Calories	377 kcal
Carbohydrates	35.3 g
Cholesterol	24.2 g
Fat	< 1 mg
Fiber	1.3 g
Protein	3.6 g
Sodium	3.6 g

* Percent Daily Values are based on a 2,000 calorie diet.

Chicken And Lemon Stir-Fry

Ingredients

- 1 lemon
- 1/2 cup reduced sodium chicken broth
- 3 tbsps reduced-sodium soy sauce
- 2 tsps cornstarch
- 1 tbsp canola oil
- 1 pound boneless skinless chicken breasts, trimmed and cut into 1-inch pieces
- 10 ounces mushrooms, halved or quartered
- 1 cup diagonally sliced carrots (1/4-inch thick)
- 2 cups snow peas, stem and strings removed
- 1 bunch scallions, cut into 1-inch pieces, white and green parts divided
- 1 tbsp chopped garlic

Directions

- Grate 1 tsp of lemon zest.

- Make 3 tsps of juiced lemon.
- Combine with 3 tbsps of broth, cornstarch, and soy sauce in a bowl.
- Get a wok and heat oil.
- Fry chicken for 5 mins. Put aside.
- Stir fry carrots and mushrooms for 5 mins. Mix in snow peas, garlic, lemon zest, and scallion whites and stir fry everything until you notice a nice aroma (30 secs to 1 min).
- Add your wet mixture from earlier and continue stir frying until thick (3 to 5 mins).
- Finally add back your chicken the scallion greens and stir fry until the chicken is cooked fully about two mins.
- Enjoy.

Servings: 4 servings

Timing Information:

Preparation	Cooking	Total Time
		40 mins

Nutritional Information:

Calories	256 kcal
Carbohydrates	16.5 g
Cholesterol	70 mg
Fat	7.7 g
Fiber	4.4 g
Protein	31.1 g
Sodium	614 mg

* Percent Daily Values are based on a 2,000 calorie diet.

A Turkey Stir-Fry

Ingredients

- 1 pound turkey meat, diced
- 2 tbsps oyster sauce, divided
- 1 (1 inch) piece fresh ginger root, finely chopped, divided
- 2 tbsps Chinese cooking wine, divided
- 1 tbsp vegetable oil
- 1 tbsp minced garlic
- 1 (11 ounce) can lychees, drained
- 2 red chile peppers, seeded and sliced into strips
- 1 tbsp soy sauce, or to taste
- 1 dash ground black pepper
- 1 bunch fresh cilantro, chopped
- 1 bunch green onions, chopped

Directions

- Get bowl and combine the following: 1 tbsp of Chinese cooking wine, 1 table of oyster sauce, and half of your ginger.

Use this to marinate your turkey for at least twenty mins.
- Get a frying pan and heat oil. Add garlic and let it fry until golden.
- Add your turkey with marinade and combine wine and ginger mix plus your oyster sauce, soy sauce, chili peppers, and lychees and cook for 5 mins.
- Add some fresh cilantro, peppers, and green onions before serving.
- Enjoy.

Servings: 4 servings

Timing Information:

Preparation	Cooking	Total Time
10 mins	10 mins	40 mins

Nutritional Information:

Calories	294 kcal
Carbohydrates	22.2 g
Cholesterol	67 mg
Fat	11.7 g
Fiber	2.7 g
Protein	25.5 g
Sodium	403 mg

* Percent Daily Values are based on a 2,000 calorie diet.

Tofu Stir Fry II

Ingredients

- 1/3 cup lite soy sauce
- 1 tbsp Thai garlic chili paste
- 2 cloves garlic, diced
- 2 tsps cayenne pepper
- 1 1/2 tsps diced fresh ginger
- 1/2 (16 ounce) package linguine-style rice noodles
- 3 tbsps olive oil
- 1 (12 ounce) package extra-firm tofu, cut into 1/2-inch cubes
- 3 green onions, minced
- 1 cup snow peas
- 1/2 green bell pepper, sliced
- 1/2 red bell pepper, sliced

Directions

- Get a bowl combine the following: ginger, soy sauce, cayenne pepper, garlic chili paste, and garlic.
- Get another bowl and fill it with hot water put your noodles in this

water let it sit covered for 10 mins until soft. After 10 mins drain them.
- Grab your frying pan and with medium heat get oil hot.
- Stir fry tofu cubes until golden (6 mins). Combine green onion and fry for another 2 mins.
- Now put one half of the wet mixture over the tofu get it simmering for 5 mins.
- Mix in green bell pepper, snow peas, and red bell pepper and stir fry until veggies are soft. 5 mins.
- Add the other half of the wet mixture and cook until the mixture is very thick and your veggies are tender but not too soft. About 5 mins.
- Mix in your noodles and get everything evenly coated. Stir frying for 3 to 5 mins.
- Let the contents cool. Enjoy.

Servings: 2 servings

Timing Information:

Preparation	Cooking	Total Time
25 mins	35 mins	1 hr

Nutritional Information:

Calories	115.2 g
Carbohydrates	834 kcal
Cholesterol	0 mg
Fat	31.3 g
Fiber	6.3 g
Protein	25.4 g
Sodium	1708 mg

* Percent Daily Values are based on a 2,000 calorie diet.

Pork Stir Fry II

Ingredients

- 5 tbsps reduced-sodium soy sauce
- 2 tbsps rice wine vinegar
- 1 tbsp cornstarch
- 2 tbsps sesame oil, divided
- 1 (1 pound) pork tenderloin, cut into strips
- 1 fresh red chile pepper, chopped
- 2 cloves garlic, minced
- 1 onion, chopped
- 1 green bell pepper, chopped
- 1 head bok choy, leaves and stalks separated, chopped
- 2 crowns broccoli, chopped
- 1 tsp ground ginger

Directions

- Get a bowl and combine the following: cornstarch, vinegar, and soy sauce.
- Get your frying pan and with a high level of heat get 1 tbsp of oil hot.

- Fry pork pieces until golden about 4 mins with high heat. Plate the meat after cooked fully.
- Add more oil to the pan and heat it.
- Stir fry for 30 secs chili pepper and garlic. Combine onion and green pepper and stir fry for 4 mins until onions are tender.
- Combine your cut bok choy with the onion and fry for 3 mins.
- Mix in broccoli and stir fry until soft about 3 mins.
- Finally add pork and mix and cut bok choy leaves and the wet soy sauce mixture from earlier, and some ginger.
- Stir fry for 8 mins until you find the bok choy leaves wilted.
- Enjoy.

Servings: 6 servings

Timing Information:

Preparation	Cooking	Total Time
25 mins	15 mins	40 mins

Nutritional Information:

Calories	188 kcal
Carbohydrates	13 g
Cholesterol	42 mg
Fat	7.8 g
Fiber	3.3 g
Protein	17.7 g
Sodium	541 mg

* Percent Daily Values are based on a 2,000 calorie diet.

Sesame Veggie Stir-Fry

Ingredients

- 1 pound broccoli
- 1/4 pound fresh snow peas, strings removed
- 1 red onion, sliced
- 3 tbsps sesame oil
- 1 red bell pepper, cut into 1/4-inch strips
- 2 tsps minced garlic
- 1/4 cup Kikkoman Less Sodium Soy Sauce
- 1/2 tbsp sesame seeds

Directions

- Cut your broccoli so that its stem is only 1 inch in length.
- Any stem that is left should be diced for faster cooking.
- Get a pot and boil some water in it. Once boiling add broccoli and snow peas let them boil for about 1 min.

- Rinse them under cool water to stop cooking process plate them for later.
- Get a frying pan and heat sesame oil.
- Stir fry the following for 1 min: snow peas, broccoli, red bell pepper, red onion, and some garlic.
- Now combine with the veggies your soy sauce and stir fry for about 2 mins.
- Finally add some sesame seeds and let everything cool before serving.
- Enjoy.

Servings: 4 servings

Timing Information:

Preparation	Cooking	Total Time
		≈ 40 mins

Nutritional Information:

Calories	191 kcal
Carbohydrates	16.9 g
Cholesterol	0 mg
Fat	11.4 g
Fiber	4.9 g
Protein	7 g
Sodium	1258 mg

* Percent Daily Values are based on a 2,000 calorie diet.

Bitter Melon Stir-Fry

Ingredients

- 2 tbsps olive oil
- 1 small onion, diced
- 2 cloves garlic, crushed
- 1/2 pound pork loin, cut into small cubes
- 1/2 pound tiger prawns, peeled and deveined
- 1 tomato, chopped
- salt and pepper to taste
- 1 bitter melon, seeded and sliced

Directions

- Get a frying pan and with a medium level of heat get your olive oil hot.
- Stir fry garlic and onions for 5 mins until aromatic.
- Combine pork and fry for 5 mins or until the pork is fully cooked.
- Combine prawns and continue stir frying for 5 mins.

- Combine with everything some salt and pepper and tomatoes fry for 5 mins.
- Let cool and serve.
- Enjoy.

Servings: 5 servings

Timing Information:

Preparation	Cooking	Total Time
20 mins	25 mins	45 mins

Nutritional Information:

Calories	159 kcal
Carbohydrates	4.5 g
Cholesterol	91 mg
Fat	8.4 g
Fiber	1.7 g
Protein	16.1 g
Sodium	97 mg

* Percent Daily Values are based on a 2,000 calorie diet.

Indian Stir-Fry

Ingredients

- 1 tbsp vegetable oil, or to taste
- 1/4 onion, chopped
- 1 clove garlic, minced
- 1 tsp curry powder, or to taste
- 1/4 tsp ground cumin
- salt and ground black pepper to taste
- 1 cup chopped asparagus
- 1/2 cup broccoli florets
- 2 tbsps water
- 3 1/2 ounces uncooked medium shrimp, peeled and deveined

Directions

- Get a frying and pan and with a medium level of heat get your oil hot.
- Stir fry your onions and garlic for 7 mins.
- Combine the following seasonings with onions: pepper, salt, cumin, and curry powder.

- Then mix into the onions your broccoli and asparagus.
- Cover the veggies with some water and cook until everything is soft for about 4 mins.
- Finally add shrimp to the veggies and stir fry until the shrimp are pink (5 mins).
- Enjoy.

Servings: 1 serving

Timing Information:

Preparation	Cooking	Total Time
15 mins	15 mins	30 mins

Nutritional Information:

Calories	262 kcal
Carbohydrates	13.2 g
Cholesterol	148 mg
Fat	15.2 g
Fiber	5.2 g
Protein	21 g
Sodium	193 mg

* Percent Daily Values are based on a 2,000 calorie diet.

Ragin' Cajun Stir-Fry

Ingredients

- 4 cups water
- 1/4 tsp salt
- 2 tbsps butter
- 3 dried red chilies, broken into several pieces
- 2 cups uncooked white rice
- 1 tbsp sesame oil
- 2 garlic cloves, minced
- 2 tbsps soy sauce, divided
- 1 skinless, boneless chicken breast half, diced
- 1 tsp dried basil
- 1 tsp ground white pepper
- 1/2 tsp dry ground mustard
- 1 pinch ground turmeric
- 1 tbsp butter
- 1 1/2 cups broccoli florets
- 1 cup diced green bell pepper
- 1 cup diced red bell pepper
- 1/2 cup diced onion
- 1 tsp lemon juice

Directions

- Get a pot and with a high level of heat mix the following: red chili peppers, 2 tbsps of butter, water, and salt. Let everything begin to simmer before continuing.
- Once boiling add rice and bring the heat down to a low level let the rice cook down until soft for about 20 mins, stirring sometimes.
- Get a frying pan heat sesame oil. Stir fry with some garlic until aromatic in the oil and pour in half of your soy sauce after 1 min.
- Stir fry the chicken in the soy sauce and garlic with the following ingredients for 8 mins: turmeric, basil, dry mustard, and white pepper.
- Add the other half of the soy sauce.
- Stir fry 1 tablespoon of butter with onion, green pepper, and broccoli in another frying pan for 10 mins until everything is soft.
- Add some lemon juice to these veggies.

- Finally mix the veggies with the chicken before letting everything cool down.
- Enjoy.

Servings: 4 servings

Timing Information:

Preparation	Cooking	Total Time
15 mins	30 mins	45 mins

Nutritional Information:

Calories	584 kcal
Carbohydrates	95 g
Cholesterol	40 mg
Fat	15.5 g
Fiber	4.2 g
Protein	17.9 g
Sodium	769 mg

* Percent Daily Values are based on a 2,000 calorie diet.

Cabbage Stir-Fry

Ingredients

- 1 tbsp vegetable oil
- 2 tbsps minced onion
- 2 cloves garlic, minced
- 6 cups chopped cabbage
- 1 tbsp soy sauce
- 1/2 tsp white sugar
- 1/8 tsp ground black pepper

Directions

- Get a frying pan heat vegie oil.
- Fry garlic and onions until soft (10 mins).
- Combine cabbage and stir fry for about 5 mins.
- Lower the heat to a low level and combine the following: black pepper, sugar, and soy sauce.
- Continue to stir fry for 5 mins before serving.
- Enjoy.

Servings: 4 servings

Timing Information:

Preparation	Cooking	Total Time
10 mins	20 mins	30 mins

Nutritional Information:

Calories	72 kcal
Carbohydrates	9.6 g
Cholesterol	0 mg
Fat	3.6 g
Fiber	3.5 g
Protein	2.1 g
Sodium	250 mg

* Percent Daily Values are based on a 2,000 calorie diet.

Bok Choy Stir-Fry

Ingredients

- 1 tbsp olive oil
- 1 clove garlic, minced, or more to taste
- 1 tsp minced fresh ginger root
- 5 heads baby bok choy, ends trimmed and leaves separated
- 2 tbsps water

Directions

- Get a frying pan and heat olive oil.
- Stir fry ginger and garlic until aromatic (1 min).
- Combine the ginger with your bok choy and put water in the pan.
- Place a lid on the pan let the bok choy wilt. This should take only 2 mins.
- Let cool and enjoy.

Servings: 2 servings

Timing Information:

Preparation	Cooking	Total Time
5 mins	5 mins	10 mins

Nutritional Information:

Calories	95 kcal
Carbohydrates	6.1 g
Cholesterol	0 mg
Fat	7.3 g
Fiber	2.6 g
Protein	3.9 g
Sodium	163 mg

* Percent Daily Values are based on a 2,000 calorie diet.

Asparagus Stir-Fry Re-Imagined

Ingredients

- 2 pounds asparagus, cut into 1-inch pieces
- 2 tsps sesame seeds
- 2 tbsps peanut oil
- 2 tsps grated fresh ginger
- 1/2 tsp salt
- 1 tsp sesame oil

Directions

- Get a pot and boil salted water.
- Add asparagus and boil for about 2 mins.
- Remove asparagus and run it under cold water. Set aside.
- Get a frying pan and fry sesame seeds without oil until they are golden about 5 mins at a medium heating level.
- Set toasted seeds aside.
- Get a frying pan and heat peanut oil. Combine asparagus and

ginger with some salt and fry everything until aromatic (5 mins).
- Let everything cool and add toasted sesame seeds before serving.
- Enjoy.

Servings: 6 servings

Timing Information:

Preparation	Cooking	Total Time
10 mins	10 mins	20 mins

Nutritional Information:

Calories	83 kcal
Carbohydrates	6.2 g
Cholesterol	0 mg
Fat	6 g
Fiber	3.2 g
Protein	3.5 g
Sodium	197 mg

* Percent Daily Values are based on a 2,000 calorie diet.

Maggie's Favorite Shrimp Stir-Fry

Ingredients

- 1/2 cup water
- 2 tbsps ketchup
- 2 tbsps soy sauce
- 2 1/2 tsps cornstarch
- 1 tsp honey
- 1 tsp Asian (toasted) sesame oil
- 1/4 tsp red pepper flakes
- 3/4 pound cooked shrimp
- 2 tbsps vegetable oil
- 2 cloves garlic, crushed
- 1 thin slice fresh ginger root
- 1 small head broccoli, broken into florets
- 1 red bell pepper, sliced
- 1 small onion, halved and sliced
- 1 small yellow squash, sliced
- 1 small zucchini, sliced
- 4 mushrooms, quartered
- 2 cups hot cooked rice

Directions

- Get a bowl and combine the following: red pepper flakes, water, and sesame oil, ketchup, honey, cornstarch and soy sauce.
- Add shrimp. Evenly coat.
- Get wok and heat veggie oil.
- Stir fry ginger and garlic for 1 min.
- Remove the garlic and ginger from the oil and throw it away.
- Stir fry the following in the seasoned oil for 5 mins: red bell peppers, mushrooms, broccoli, zucchini, onion, and yellow squash.
- Combine shrimp, veggies, and all liquid. Stir fry over high heat for 5 mins.
- Serve with rice.
- Enjoy.

Servings: 4 servings

Timing Information:

Preparation	Cooking	Total Time
30 mins	15 mins	45 mins

Nutritional Information:

Calories	337 kcal
Carbohydrates	39 g
Cholesterol	166 mg
Fat	9.7 g
Fiber	4 g
Protein	24.3 g
Sodium	756 mg

* Percent Daily Values are based on a 2,000 calorie diet.

Ginger Pork Stir Fry

Ingredients

- 4 center cut pork chops, thinly sliced
- 1/4 C. mirin
- 1/4 C. rice vinegar
- 1/2 C. soy sauce
- 1/2 C. mushrooms, sliced
- 1 green bell pepper, sliced
- 1 bunch green onions
- 1 clove garlic, minced
- 1 tbsp minced fresh ginger root
- 1 tbsp sesame oil

Directions

- Cut your pork into very thin strips while the meat is somewhat frozen.
- Get a bowl, combine: soy sauce, pork, rice vinegar, and mirin.

- Place a covering of plastic on the bowl and put the mix in the fridge.
- Now cut the following and place the mix in a 2nd bowl: green parts of the green onions, mushrooms, and the green peppers.
- Get a 3rd bowl, cut: ginger, garlic, and the white parts of the green onions.
- Now get your sesame oil hot, in a wok, then begin to stir fry the contents of your 3rd bowl for 2 mins then turn up the heat and add in the pork.
- Keep the marinade to the side and cook the pork for 5 mins.
- Now add the contents of the 2 bowl into the mix.
- Continue stir frying everything for 5 more mins then pour in the marinade and cook the contents for 3 mins.
- Enjoy.

Servings: 4 servings

Timing Information:

Preparation	Cooking	Total Time
20 m	15 m	35 m

Nutritional Information:

Calories	287 kcal
Fat	11.5 g
Carbohydrates	14.1g
Protein	28.2 g
Cholesterol	76 mg
Sodium	1869 mg

* Percent Daily Values are based on a 2,000 calorie diet.

Mediterranean Stir-Fry

Ingredients

- 2 tbsps olive oil
- 1 tbsp diced fresh oregano
- 1 tbsp diced fresh basil
- 1 clove garlic, crushed
- ground black pepper to taste
- 1 (15 oz.) can garbanzo beans, drained and rinsed
- 1 large zucchini, halved and sliced
- 1/2 C. sliced mushrooms
- 1 tbsp diced fresh cilantro
- 1 tomato, diced

Directions

- Fry the following for 10 mins in oil: pepper, oregano, zucchini, basil, garbanzos, and garlic.
- Now add in the cilantro and the mushrooms.

- Cook everything until they are soft.
- Now add in the tomatoes and place a lid on the pan.
- Cook the mix for 2 more mins then serve.
- Enjoy.

Servings: 4 servings

Timing Information:

Preparation	Cooking	Total Time
15 m	30 m	45 m

Nutritional Information:

Calories	167 kcal
Fat	7.7 g
Carbohydrates	21.2g
Protein	4.6 g
Cholesterol	0 mg
Sodium	216 mg

* Percent Daily Values are based on a 2,000 calorie diet.

Chicken and Garlic

Ingredients

- 2 tbsps peanut oil
- 6 cloves garlic, minced
- 1 tsp grated fresh ginger
- 1 bunch green onions, diced
- 1 tsp salt
- 1 lb boneless skinless chicken breasts, cut into strips
- 2 onions, thinly sliced
- 1 C. sliced cabbage
- 1 red bell pepper, thinly sliced
- 2 C. sugar snap peas
- 1 C. chicken broth
- 2 tbsps soy sauce
- 2 tbsps white sugar
- 2 tbsps cornstarch

Directions

- Get your peanut oil hot. Then add in: salt, 2 pieces of garlic, green onions, and ginger root.
- Cook this mix for 4 mins then add the chicken and cook everything for 4 more mins.
- Combine 1/2 C. broth, the rest of the garlic, peas, sweet onions, bell peppers, and cabbage. Then place a lid on the pot.
- Get a bowl, combine: cornstarch, 1/2 C. broth, sugar, and soy sauce.
- Pour this into the cabbage mix and stir the contents to coat all the ingredients.
- Cook this mix for 2 more mins then serve.
- Enjoy.

Servings: 4 servings

Timing Information:

Preparation	Cooking	Total Time
10 m	20 m	40 m

Nutritional Information:

Calories	337 kcal
Fat	8.6 g
Carbohydrates	32.3g
Protein	31.7 g
Cholesterol	67 mg
Sodium	1364 mg

* Percent Daily Values are based on a 2,000 calorie diet.

Lemon and Shrimp Stir Fry

(Paleo Approved)

Ingredients

- 1/2 C. lemon juice
- 1 small onion, finely diced
- 1/2 C. olive oil
- 3 cloves garlic, minced
- 1 tbsp lemon zest
- 1 tbsp grated ginger
- 1 tsp ground turmeric
- 24 large shrimp, peeled and deveined
- 1 tbsp coconut oil, or as needed

Directions

- Get a bowl, combine: turmeric, lemon juice, ginger, onion, lemon zest, garlic, and olive oil.
- Add in the shrimp and stir the contents.

- Now place a covering of plastic on the bowl and put everything in the fridge for 8 hrs.
- Separate the shrimp from the marinade and reserve the liquid.
- Now get your wok hot with coconut oil.
- Add in the shrimp and cook the mix for 7 mins then add in the marinade and get everything boiling while stirring.
- Once the mix has boiled for 60 secs serve it.
- Enjoy.

Servings: 4 servings

Timing Information:

Preparation	Cooking	Total Time
20 m	10 m	8 h 30 m

Nutritional Information:

Calories	388 kcal
Fat	31.7 g
Carbohydrates	5.9 g
Protein	21.1 g
Cholesterol	192 mg
Sodium	222 mg

* Percent Daily Values are based on a 2,000 calorie diet.

CHINESE SKIRT STEAK STIR FRY

Ingredients

- 1/4 C. peanut oil
- 2 tbsps soy sauce
- 1 tsp ground black pepper
- 1 lb skirt steak, sliced into strips
- 1/2 green bell pepper, diced
- 1/4 onion, diced
- 2 tbsps diced green onion
- 1 tbsp diced fresh ginger root
- 1 tbsp diced serrano pepper
- 1 C. fresh baby spinach
- 1/4 C. balsamic vinaigrette salad dressing

Directions

- Get a bowl, combine: pepper, peanut oil, and soy sauce.
- Now add in the steak and stir the contents.

- Place a covering on the bowl and put everything in the fridge overnight.
- Add the steak and the marinade to a hot wok and begin to stir fry the mix for 3 mins then add in: serrano, bell peppers, ginger, onion, and green onions.
- Once the steak is done serve the mix with the spinach and balsamic.
- Enjoy.

Servings: 2 servings

Timing Information:

Preparation	Cooking	Total Time
20 m	10 m	12 h 30 m

Nutritional Information:

Calories	620 kcal
Fat	52.5 g
Carbohydrates	9.3g
Protein	28.9 g
Cholesterol	71 mg
Sodium	1337 mg

* Percent Daily Values are based on a 2,000 calorie diet.

Pork and Tofu Stir Fry

Ingredients

- 1 C. uncooked long grain white rice
- 2 C. water
- 2 tbsps vegetable oil
- 2 cloves garlic, minced
- 1/2 lb ground pork
- 6 fresh shiitake mushrooms, diced
- 1 (14 oz.) package cubed firm tofu
- 1 green onion, thinly sliced
- 1 tbsp Asian chili pepper sauce (sriracha)
- 1 tbsp ketchup
- 2 tbsps tamari

Directions

- Get your rice boiling in water.
- Once the mix is boiling, place a lid on the pot, set the heat to a

low level, and cook everything for 22 mins.
- At the same time begin to get your oil hot in a wok and once it is, begin to stir fry your garlic for 2 mins then add in the pork and cook the mix for 6 more mins.
- Now combine in: the green onion, tamari, ketchup, and chili pepper sauce, tofu, and mushrooms.
- Continue stir frying for about 2 mins or until everything is hot and layer your rice on a serving plate with a topping of the mushroom mix.
- Enjoy.

Servings: 4 servings

Timing Information:

Preparation	Cooking	Total Time
15 m	30 m	45 m

Nutritional Information:

Calories	524 kcal
Fat	24.1 g
Carbohydrates	47.1g
Protein	31.2 g
Cholesterol	37 mg
Sodium	596 mg

* Percent Daily Values are based on a 2,000 calorie diet.

Indian Style Tofu with Lime Stir Fry

Ingredients

- 2 tbsps peanut oil
- 1 (16 oz.) package extra-firm tofu, cut into bite-sized cubes
- 1 tbsp minced fresh ginger root
- 2 tbsps red curry paste
- 1 lb zucchini, diced
- 1 red bell pepper, diced
- 3 tbsps lime juice
- 3 tbsps soy sauce
- 2 tbsps maple syrup
- 1 (14 oz.) can coconut milk
- 1/2 C. diced fresh basil

Directions

- Get your peanut oil hot and then begin to fry your tofu until it is brown. Once the tofu is evenly browned place it in a bowl.

- Add the curry paste and ginger into the wok and cook the mix for 60 secs then add in the bell peppers and zucchini.
- Cook this mix for 2 mins then add in: tofu, lime juice, coconut milk, soy sauce, and syrup.
- Get everything gently boiling for 3 mins until the veggies are soft.
- Now add in the basil and serve.
- Enjoy.

Servings: 4 servings

Timing Information:

Preparation	Cooking	Total Time
20 m	10 m	30 m

Nutritional Information:

Calories	425 kcal
Fat	38.8 g
Carbohydrates	20.9g
Protein	18.4 g
Cholesterol	0 mg
Sodium	856 mg

* Percent Daily Values are based on a 2,000 calorie diet.

Grapes and Chicken

Ingredients

- 1 tbsp vegetable oil
- 1 C. sliced red grapes
- 1 C. cubed cooked chicken
- 2 C. cooked rice
- 1/4 C. chicken broth

Directions

- Stir fry your chicken and grapes in hot veggie oil for 4 mins.
- Now add the broth and rice.
- Let the contents cook for 4 more mins until everything is hot.
- Enjoy.

Servings: 4 servings

Timing Information:

Preparation	Cooking	Total Time
15 m	10 m	25 m

Nutritional Information:

Calories	226 kcal
Fat	6.5 g
Carbohydrates	29.4g
Protein	12 g
Cholesterol	26 mg
Sodium	23 mg

* Percent Daily Values are based on a 2,000 calorie diet.

Easy Hawaiian Stir Fry

Ingredients

- 1 tbsp olive oil
- 1 (2 lb) ham steak, cubed
- 1 onion, diced
- 1 (15 oz.) can pineapple chunks with juice, divided
- 1 apple, cored and diced
- 1 tbsp brown sugar
- salt and pepper to taste

Directions

- Stir fry your onions and ham in oil for 7 mins then add in half of the pineapple juice and cook the contents for 3 more mins.
- Now add the pineapple pieces, some brown sugar and the apples.
- Stir fry the contents for 7 mins then add some pepper and salt.

- Enjoy.

Servings: 3 servings

Timing Information:

Preparation	Cooking	Total Time
20 m	15 m	35 m

Nutritional Information:

Calories	768 kcal
Fat	29.9 g
Carbohydrates	36.5g
Protein	85.3 g
Cholesterol	1212 mg
Sodium	8161 mg

* Percent Daily Values are based on a 2,000 calorie diet.

MEXICAN STYLE PORK STIR FRY

Ingredients

- 1/4 C. olive oil
- 1/2 C. finely diced fresh cilantro leaves
- 1 tbsp finely diced ginger
- 4 cloves garlic, finely diced
- 1 lb pork tenderloin, thinly sliced
- 2 tbsps olive oil, divided
- 2 onions, thinly sliced
- 1 red bell pepper, thinly sliced
- 1 tbsp lime juice
- 1/2 C. diced fresh cilantro

Directions

- Get a bowl, combine: garlic, 1/4 C. olive oil, ginger, and 1/2 C. cilantro.
- Combine in the pork and place a covering of plastic around the bowl.

- Place everything in the fridge for 8 hrs.
- Begin to stir fry the pork in 1 tbsp of olive oil for 12 mins and remove it from the pan.
- Now add in 1 more tbsp of oil and the onions.
- Cook this mix for 5 mins then add in the bell peppers and cook everything for 5 more mins.
- Now add the pork back into the mix as well as a 1/2 C. of cilantro and the lime juice.
- Continue stir frying for 2 mins then serve.
- Enjoy.

Servings: 4 servings

Timing Information:

Preparation	Cooking	Total Time
30 m	15 m	8 h 45 m

Nutritional Information:

Calories	308 kcal
Fat	18 g
Carbohydrates	14.4g
Protein	22.4 g
Cholesterol	63 mg
Sodium	56 mg

* Percent Daily Values are based on a 2,000 calorie diet.

Every Pepper Stir Fry

Ingredients

- 1 large yellow bell pepper, seeded and diced
- 1/2 large red bell pepper, seeded and diced
- 1/2 small head cabbage, diced
- 1 small head purple cauliflower, diced
- 1 small onion, diced
- 1 C. water
- 1/2 lb boneless chuck, cut into 1-inch cubes
- 2 tbsps olive oil, divided
- 1 large orange - peeled, sectioned, and cut into large pieces
- 1 tbsp grated orange zest
- 1 large green onion, diced
- 1/3 C. teriyaki sauce
- 1 tbsp oyster sauce

Directions

- Get a saucepan and combine: onion, water, cauliflower, bell peppers, and cabbage.
- Place a lid on the pot and steam the veggies for 12 mins.
- Now flatten your chunks to half an inch then cut each one into 4 pieces.
- Begin to stir fry the meat in 1 tbsp of olive oil, until browned all over, then place the meat to the side.
- Add in the rest of the olive oil and begin to fry the green onions, zest, and orange for 4 mins.
- Combine the meat with the veggies as well as the oranges, and top the mix with the oyster sauce and teriyaki.
- Cook everything for 2 more mins while stirring.
- Enjoy.

Servings: 4 servings

Timing Information:

Preparation	Cooking	Total Time
25 m	25 m	50 m

Nutritional Information:

Calories	315 kcal
Fat	18.6 g
Carbohydrates	24.6g
Protein	15 g
Cholesterol	41 mg
Sodium	1027 mg

* Percent Daily Values are based on a 2,000 calorie diet.

COUSCOUS AND CAULIFLOWER STIR FRY

Ingredients

- 1 1/2 C. water
- 1 C. couscous
- 2 C. chicken broth
- 1/4 C. cornstarch
- 3 tbsps soy sauce
- 3 tbsps brown sugar
- 1/8 tsp ground ginger
- 1 tbsp vegetable oil
- 2 cloves garlic, minced
- 1 (16 oz.) package mixed broccoli and cauliflower florets
- 1 carrot, sliced
- 1/4 lb cooked ham, cut into strips
- 1 (8 oz.) can sliced water chestnuts, drained
- 1/2 C. sliced almonds

Directions

- Get your couscous and water boiling, set the heat to low, and gently cook the couscous for 12 mins.
- Now place a lid on the pot and put everything to the side.
- Get a bowl, combine: ginger, broth, brown sugar, soy sauce, and cornstarch.
- Get your oil hot, in a wok, and begin to stir fry your carrots, garlic, cauliflower, and broccoli for 10 mins.
- Now add in the broth mix as well as the water chestnuts and the ham.
- Cook everything for 3 mins then add the almonds and serve the mix with the couscous.
- Enjoy.

Servings: 6 servings

Timing Information:

Preparation	Cooking	Total Time
10 m	10 m	20 m

Nutritional Information:

Calories	318 kcal
Fat	8.9 g
Carbohydrates	46.6g
Protein	12.9 g
Cholesterol	11 mg
Sodium	994 mg

* Percent Daily Values are based on a 2,000 calorie diet.

Easy Eggplant and Spinach Stir Fry

Ingredients

- 1/2 large eggplant, sliced into rounds
- 1/8 tsp salt
- 4 skinless, boneless chicken breast halves , cut into cubes
- 2 cloves garlic, minced
- 2 tbsps soy sauce
- 1 tbsp canola oil
- 2 C. mushrooms, sliced
- 1/8 tsp ground black pepper
- 4 C. spinach

Directions

- Coat your eggplant pieces with salt and place them to the side for 7 mins.
- Now slice the pieces into cubes.

- Begin to stir fry your soy sauce, garlic, and chicken for 12 mins then add in some black pepper and the mushrooms.
- Let this mix cook for 4 mins.
- Now in another pan brown your eggplant in canola oil then combine the veggies with the chicken.
- Add the spinach and cook the contents for 4 mins then serve.
- Enjoy.

Servings: 4 servings

Timing Information:

Preparation	Cooking	Total Time
20 m	15 m	40 m

Nutritional Information:

Calories	190 kcal
Fat	6.3 g
Carbohydrates	8.7g
Protein	25.8 g
Cholesterol	59 mg
Sodium	600 mg

* Percent Daily Values are based on a 2,000 calorie diet.

Watermelon and Pepper Stir-Fry

Ingredients

- 1 tbsp peanut oil
- 1 onion, thinly sliced
- 3 cloves garlic, minced
- 1 tsp salt
- 1 C. peeled and sliced watermelon rind
- 1 red bell pepper, sliced thin
- 1 C. vegetable broth, divided
- 1/4 C. teriyaki sauce
- 2 tbsps cornstarch

Directions

- Begin to stir fry your salt, garlic, and onion in peanut oil for 3 mins then add half of the veggie broth, bell peppers, and the watermelon rinds.

- Now set the heat to low and let the contents cook for 7 mins.
- Get a bowl, combine: cornstarch, teriyaki, and veggie broth.
- Add this mix with the onion mix and continue heating everything until it all begins to thicken.
- Enjoy.

Servings: 4 servings

Timing Information:

Preparation	Cooking	Total Time
15 m	15 m	30 m

Nutritional Information:

Calories	116 kcal
Fat	3.8 g
Carbohydrates	18.3g
Protein	2.6 g
Cholesterol	0 mg
Sodium	1391 mg

* Percent Daily Values are based on a 2,000 calorie diet.

Down South Stir Fry

Ingredients

- 1 tbsp oil
- 1 Smithfield(R) Portobello Mushroom Marinated Fresh Pork Loin Filet, cut into thin strips
- 1 tsp dried thyme leaves
- 1/2 tsp minced garlic
- 1 medium sweet yellow onion, thinly sliced
- 1 medium red bell pepper, thinly sliced
- 1 (10 oz.) package frozen baby cob corn, thawed and drained
- 1 (10 oz.) package frozen sliced okra, thawed and drained
- 2 tbsps diced fresh parsley
- Hot pepper sauce (optional)

Directions

- Stir fry your garlic, thyme, and pork in hot oil until the pork is fully done, then add in the okra, onions, corn, and red pepper.
- Continue stir frying the mix until your onion is soft and browned.
- Now add the hot sauce and parsley.
- Enjoy.

Servings: 4 servings

Timing Information:

Preparation	Cooking	Total Time
10 m	10 m	20 m

Nutritional Information:

Calories	375 kcal
Fat	14.4 g
Carbohydrates	29.6g
Protein	36.6 g
Cholesterol	85 mg
Sodium	460 mg

* Percent Daily Values are based on a 2,000 calorie diet.

Vietnamese Stir-Fry

Ingredients

- 1/4 C. olive oil
- 4 cloves garlic, minced
- 1 (1 inch) piece fresh ginger root, minced
- 1/4 C. fish sauce
- 1/4 C. reduced-sodium soy sauce
- 1 dash sesame oil
- 2 lbs sirloin tip, thinly sliced
- 1 tbsp vegetable oil
- 2 cloves garlic, minced
- 3 green onions, cut into 2 inch pieces
- 1 large onion, thinly sliced
- 2 C. frozen whole green beans, partially thawed
- 1/2 C. reduced-sodium beef broth
- 2 tbsps lime juice
- 1 tbsp diced fresh Thai basil
- 1 tbsp diced fresh mint
- 1 pinch red pepper flakes, or to taste

- 1/2 tsp ground black pepper
- 1/4 C. diced fresh cilantro

Directions

- Get a bowl, combine: sesame oil, olive oil, soy sauce, 4 pieces of garlic, fish sauce, and ginger.
- Combine in the beef and place a covering of plastic around the bowl.
- Put everything in the fridge for 4 hrs.
- Stir fry your beef in hot veggie oil until it is fully done then place it to the side.
- Set the heat under the wok to low and add in some more oil.
- Begin to fry: the onions, green onions, and 2 pieces of garlic.
- Cook the onions for 7 mins then add: black pepper, green beans, pepper flakes, beef broth, mint, lime juice, and basil.

- Now add the beef back into the mix and the cilantro as well. Get everything hot and then serve.
- Enjoy.

Servings: 6 servings

Timing Information:

Preparation	Cooking	Total Time
30 m	25 m	2 h 55 m

Nutritional Information:

Calories	475 kcal
Fat	34.4 g
Carbohydrates	8.8g
Protein	31.7 g
Cholesterol	101 mg
Sodium	1174 mg

* Percent Daily Values are based on a 2,000 calorie diet.

Filipino Style Steak Stir Fry

Ingredients

- 2 (1/2 lb) New York strip steaks, sliced into thin strips
- 2 tbsps cornstarch
- 2 tbsps soy sauce
- 1 1/2 tsps white sugar
- 3 tbsps olive oil
- 1 sweet onion, diced
- 2 cloves garlic, crushed
- 1 tbsp oyster sauce
- salt and pepper to taste
- 1 lb snow peas
- 3/4 C. green peas
- 1 carrot, sliced
- 2 stalks celery, sliced
- 1 red bell pepper, seeded and cut into chunks
- 1/4 C. oil for deep frying

Directions

- Coat your pieces of steak with cornstarch in a bowl.
- Get a 2nd bowl, combine: sugar and soy sauce.
- Combine both bowls and toss the mix evenly.
- Place a covering of plastic around the bowl and put everything in the fridge for 4 hours.
- Begin to stir fry your garlic and onions in 3 tbsp of olive oil for 9 mins then add the oyster sauce and some pepper and salt.
- Combine in the bell peppers, snow peas, celery, green peas, and carrots.
- Continue stir frying this mix for 12 mins. Then place the veggies to the side.
- Now add in two more 2 tbsps of oil, and begin to fry your beef for 6 mins per side and then combine in the veggies and get everything hot.
- Enjoy.

Servings: 4 servings

Timing Information:

Preparation	Cooking	Total Time
30 m	30 m	3 h

Nutritional Information:

Calories	452 kcal
Fat	20.6 g
Carbohydrates	26.5g
Protein	39.1 g
Cholesterol	66 mg
Sodium	613 mg

* Percent Daily Values are based on a 2,000 calorie diet.

Chicken and Spaghetti Stir Fry

Ingredients

- 8 oz. spaghetti
- 2 cloves crushed garlic
- 2 tbsps olive oil
- 1 onion, sliced into thin rings
- 2 skinless, boneless chicken breast halves - cut into bite-size pieces
- 2 C. broccoli florets
- 2 C. cauliflower florets
- 2 C. julienned carrots
- salt to taste
- ground black pepper to taste
- 2 tbsps soy sauce

Directions

- Boil your pasta in water and salt for 9 mins then remove all the liquids.

- At the same time, as the pasta cooks, begin to stir fry your garlic for 2 mins in oil.
- Then add the onions and continue cooking the onions until they are tender.
- Now add the chicken and fry the contents until the chicken is fully done.
- Once the chicken is done add: the carrots, cauliflower, and broccoli.
- Let everything cook for 7 mins then top the mix with pepper, salt, and soy sauce.
- Combine the veggies with the pasta and serve.
- Enjoy.

Servings: 4 servings

Timing Information:

Preparation	Cooking	Total Time
20 m	25 m	45 m

Nutritional Information:

Calories	403 kcal
Fat	8.7 g
Carbohydrates	57g
Protein	24.7 g
Cholesterol	34 mg
Sodium	566 mg

* Percent Daily Values are based on a 2,000 calorie diet.

Caribbean Stir Fry

Ingredients

- 1/4 C. butter
- 1 tsp cumin seeds
- 4 large skinless, boneless chicken breast halves, thinly sliced
- 2 tbsps vegetable oil
- 1 large onion, finely diced
- 2 large carrots, thinly sliced
- 4 cloves garlic, diced
- 1 tbsp grated ginger
- 2 tsps crushed red pepper flakes
- 1 tsp honey
- 1 tsp ground cumin
- 1/2 tsp ground cinnamon
- 1/2 tsp curry powder, or more to taste
- salt and ground black pepper to taste
- 1 (14 oz.) can coconut milk

Directions

- Toast your cumin in butter for 2 mins, while stirring, then add the chicken.
- Cook the meat until it is fully done for about 9 mins. Then add some veggie oil to the pan and: black pepper, onion, salt, carrots, curry powder, garlic, cinnamon, ginger, ground cumin, pepper flakes, and honey.
- Let this mix cook for 10 mins then add the coconut milk and get everything simmering.
- Let the contents continue to cook for 8 more mins and stir the mix occasionally.
- Enjoy.

Servings: 4 servings

Timing Information:

Preparation	Cooking	Total Time
25 m	30 m	55 m

Nutritional Information:

Calories	657 kcal
Fat	45.3 g
Carbohydrates	14.2g
Protein	50.6 g
Cholesterol	1160 mg
Sodium	156 mg

* Percent Daily Values are based on a 2,000 calorie diet.

Maggie's Easy Shrimp and Garlic

Ingredients

- 1 C. chicken stock
- 1 tbsp reduced-sodium soy sauce
- 1 tbsp cornstarch
- 1 tbsp minced garlic
- salt and ground black pepper to taste
- 3 tbsps sesame oil
- 1 (16 oz.) package frozen stir-fry vegetables
- 20 uncooked medium shrimp, peeled and deveined

Directions

- Get a bowl, combine: pepper, garlic, chicken stock, salt, cornstarch, and soy sauce.

- Now get your sesame oil hot and begin to stir fry your veggies for 6 mins.
- Add in the shrimp and cook the mix for 4 mins.
- Pour in the cornstarch mix and cook the contents for 7 more mins before serving.
- Enjoy.

Servings: 4 servings

Timing Information:

Preparation	Cooking	Total Time
10 m	15 m	25 m

Nutritional Information:

Calories	169 kcal
Fat	10.9 g
Carbohydrates	11.8g
Protein	8 g
Cholesterol	46 mg
Sodium	636 mg

* Percent Daily Values are based on a 2,000 calorie diet.

Ginger Tofu with Peanut Sauce

Ingredients

- 1 tsp vegetable oil
- 1 (16 oz.) package frozen stir-fry vegetables
- 1/2 tsp minced fresh ginger
- salt and pepper to taste
- 2 eggs, beaten
- 1 C. cornstarch
- salt and pepper to taste
- 1 (14 oz.) package firm tofu, drained and cubed
- 1/2 C. vegetable oil
- 3/4 C. peanut sauce
- 1/4 C. diced peanuts

Directions

- Stir fry your veggies in hot oil until they are soft then add in some pepper, salt, and the ginger.

- Cook the mix for 2 more mins then place everything to the side.
- Whisk your eggs in a bowl.
- Get a 2nd bowl, combine: pepper, salt, and cornstarch.
- Coat your pieces of tofu first with egg and then with the cornstarch.
- Add the rest of the oil to the pan and fry your tofu pieces for 6 mins then add the peanuts and the peanut sauce.
- Continue stir frying the mix for 3 more mins.
- Enjoy.

Servings: 8 servings

Timing Information:

Preparation	Cooking	Total Time
15 m	15 m	30 m

Nutritional Information:

Calories	417 kcal
Fat	28.7 g
Carbohydrates	27.4g
Protcin	15.2 g
Cholesterol	47 mg
Sodium	812 mg

* Percent Daily Values are based on a 2,000 calorie diet.

Orange Chicken and Broccoli II

Ingredients

- 1/2 C. orange juice
- 3 tbsps soy sauce
- 3 cloves garlic, diced
- 1 tbsp grated orange zest
- 1 tsp ground ginger
- 1/2 tsp red pepper flakes (optional)
- 3 tbsps vegetable oil
- 4 skinless, boneless chicken breast halves, thinly sliced
- 1/2 C. chicken broth
- 2 tbsps cornstarch
- 1 (16 oz.) package frozen stir-fry vegetables
- 1 C. sugar snap peas
- 1 C. broccoli florets
- 1 C. sliced carrot

Directions

- Get a bowl, combine: pepper flakes, orange juice, ginger, soy sauce, orange zest, and garlic.
- Get your oil hot and then begin to stir fry your chicken and orange mix for 12 mins.
- Get a 2nd bowl, combine: cornstarch and broth.
- Add this mix to the chicken, gradually, to make the sauce thicker.
- Once the mix has reached a consistency that you prefer add: carrots, veggies, broccoli, and snap peas.
- Continue frying and stirring the contents for 9 more mins.
- Enjoy.

Servings: 4 servings

Timing Information:

Preparation	Cooking	Total Time
20 m	20 m	40 m

Nutritional Information:

Calories	380 kcal
Fat	14 g
Carbohydrates	33.1g
Protein	31.7 g
Cholesterol	68 mg
Sodium	938 mg

* Percent Daily Values are based on a 2,000 calorie diet.

Chinese Pork

Ingredients

- 1 lb boneless pork chops, cut into stir-fry strips
- 1 tbsp hoisin sauce
- 1 tbsp cornstarch
- 2 tbsps hoisin sauce
- 1/4 C. chicken broth
- 1 tbsp cornstarch
- 1 tbsp rice vinegar
- 1 tbsp white sugar
- 1 tsp red pepper flakes, or to taste
- 1 tbsp sesame oil
- 2 cloves garlic, minced
- 2 tsps minced fresh ginger root
- 1 carrot, peeled and sliced
- 1 green bell pepper, sliced
- 1 (4 oz.) can sliced water chestnuts, drained
- 2 green onions, sliced

Directions

- Get a bowl, combine: 1 tbsp cornstarch, pork, and 1 tbsp hoisin.
- Get a 2nd bowl, combine: cayenne, the rest of the hoisin, sugar, broth, rice wine vinegar, and 1 tbsp of cornstarch.
- Now get your sesame oil hot and begin to stir fry your pork for 7 mins.
- Add in the water chestnuts, bell peppers, and carrots.
- Cook everything until the veggies are soft then add the contents of the 2nd bowl.
- Cook the mix for 5 more mins.
- Enjoy.

Servings: 4 servings

Timing Information:

Preparation	Cooking	Total Time
30 m	20 m	50 m

Nutritional Information:

Calories	236 kcal
Fat	11.4 g
Carbohydrates	17.5g
Protein	15.6 g
Cholesterol	39 mg
Sodium	295 mg

* Percent Daily Values are based on a 2,000 calorie diet.

Easy Stir Fry Lo Mein

Ingredients

- 4 skinless, boneless chicken breast halves - cut into thin strips
- 5 tsps white sugar, divided
- 3 tbsps rice wine vinegar
- 1/2 C. soy sauce, divided
- 1 1/4 C. chicken broth
- 1 C. water
- 1 tbsp sesame oil
- 1/2 tsp ground black pepper
- 2 tbsps cornstarch
- 1 (12 oz.) package uncooked linguine pasta
- 2 tbsps vegetable oil, divided
- 2 tbsps minced fresh ginger root
- 1 tbsp minced garlic
- 1/2 lb fresh shiitake mushrooms, stemmed and sliced
- 6 green onions, sliced diagonally into 1/2 inch pieces

Directions

- Get a bowl, mix: 1/4 C. soy sauce, chicken, 1.5 tbsps vinegar, and 2.5 tsps sugar.
- Place a covering of plastic around the bowl and put everything in the fridge for 60 mins.
- Get a 2nd bowl, mix: black pepper, broth, sesame oil, and water.
- Now combine both bowls.
- Get a 3rd bowl and mix a small amount of the contents from the 2nd bowl with your cornstarch until everything is smooth.
- Then combine everything together into 1 bowl.
- Boil your pasta in water and salt for 9 mins, then remove all the liquids.
- At the same time begin to stir fry your chicken in 1 tbsp of veggie oil for 6 mins and then place it to the side.
- Add in the rest of the oil and fry the following for 2 mins: green

onions, ginger mushrooms, and garlic.
- Combine in the cornstarch mix and the chicken and cook everything for 3 mins until it all becomes thick.
- Now add the pasta and toss the contents.
- Enjoy.

Servings: 4 servings

Timing Information:

Preparation	Cooking	Total Time
45 m	30 m	2 h 15 m

Nutritional Information:

Calories	603 kcal
Fat	14.9 g
Carbohydrates	78.9g
Protein	38.3 g
Cholesterol	62 mg
Sodium	2177 mg

* Percent Daily Values are based on a 2,000 calorie diet.

Ginger Chicken with Apricots

Ingredients

- 1 (15 oz.) can apricot halves, drained and diced, juice reserved
- 2 tbsps soy sauce
- 1 tbsp cornstarch
- 1/2 tsp garlic powder
- 1/2 tsp onion powder
- 1/2 tsp crushed red pepper flakes
- 2 tbsps vegetable oil
- 1 tbsp minced fresh ginger root
- 1 lb skinless, boneless chicken breast meat - cut into strips
- 1 (16 oz.) package frozen stir-fry vegetables, thawed
- 1 (8 oz.) can pineapple chunks, drained
- 3 green onion, sliced

Directions

- Get a bowl, combine: pepper flakes, apricot juice, onion powder, soy sauce, garlic powder, and cornstarch.
- Begin to stir fry your ginger in veggie oil until it browns, for about 30 secs.
- Now add the chicken and cook the meat until it is halfway done.
- Add the stir fry veggies and continue cooking everything until the veggies are soft and the chicken is fully done.
- Now add the cornstarch mix, apricots, and pineapple and get everything boiling while stirring and cooking the mix for 2 mins.
- Garnish the dish with your green onions and serve.
- Enjoy.

Servings: 6 servings

Timing Information:

Preparation	Cooking	Total Time
25 m	15 m	40 m

Nutritional Information:

Calories	220 kcal
Fat	6.6 g
Carbohydrates	23.2g
Protein	18.7 g
Cholesterol	43 mg
Sodium	529 mg

* Percent Daily Values are based on a 2,000 calorie diet.

Thanks for Reading! Now Let's Try some Sushi and Dump Dinners....

Send the Book!

To grab this **box set** simply follow the link mentioned above, or tap the book cover.

This will take you to a page where you can simply enter your email address and a PDF version of the **box set** will be emailed to you.

I hope you are ready for some serious cooking!

[Send the Book!](#)

You will also receive updates about all my new books when they are free.

Also don't forget to like and subscribe on the social networks. I love meeting my readers. Links to all my profiles are below so please click and connect :)

[Facebook](#)

[Twitter](#)

Come On...
Let's Be Friends :)

I adore my readers and love connecting with them socially. Please follow the links below so we can connect on Facebook, Twitter, and Google+.

Facebook

Twitter

I also have a blog that I regularly update for my readers so check it out below.

My Blog

Can I Ask A Favour?

If you found this book interesting, or have otherwise found any benefit in it. Then may I ask that you post a review of it on Amazon? Nothing excites me more than new reviews, especially reviews which suggest new topics for writing. I do read all reviews and I always factor feedback into my newer works.

So if you are willing to take ten minutes to write what you sincerely thought about this book then please visit our Amazon page and post your opinions.

Again thank you!

Interested in Other Easy Cookbooks?

Everything is easy! Check out my Amazon Author page for more great cookbooks:

For a complete listing of all my books please see my author page.